Living in -2- Worlds

A True Story.

Jeff McBride

Living in -2- Worlds.
A True Story.
by Jeff McBride

Printed in the United States of America

ISBN 9781613796283

www.xulonpress.com

I present this story to those of you who have lived a similar life, and to all of those who are aware there is something more out there. A life that at times may seem slightly out of step with everyone and everything that surrounds you. I hope these words bring comfort, understanding and joy to all of you who read this.

Jeff

About the author

J eff McBride is a clairvoyant who has spent his life developing his abilities.

He has learned to use these abilities throughout his many life changes. These changes include, but are not limited to, being a successful business owner, a police officer on both ends of the USA and a father.

He has been actively involved in missing person's cases.

He has been in movies, commercials, soap operas and has had many national modeling ads. He is a member of the Screen Actors Guild and AFTRA.

He is a record setting bodybuilder and has held many titles in this sport.

The information he has obtained through the years has allowed him to move forward in all his desired fields.

Find out even more at WWW.Jeffreyjohn26.com his personal site. There you will find contact links and upcoming appearance locations and dates.

Contents

From The Beginning

Chapter 1

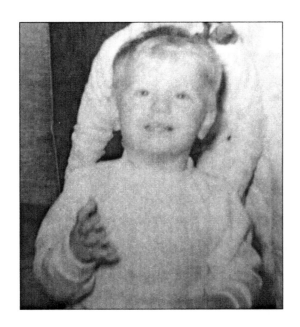

From what I have been told and from the medical records pertaining to my childhood, I learned I was born into a family whose children all had blood issues at birth. My sisters and I were born with RH positive blood, which was transfused at birth. The blood transfusion at birth caused a period of incubation. I also learned that I was born about six weeks early. I was in a big rush to get started I guess.

Shortly after arriving home from the hospital, I was having trouble with my stomach. I was told that I would eat like a healthy, hungry baby, but shortly after eating, I would vomit all that was taken in. My parents told me they would feed me and put me into a bassinette. Then after a short time passed, I would vomit. The force of the vomiting was so strong they said, it would come right out of the bassinette.

This cycle of illness would continue for weeks. They would change formulas, and the doctor told them it was normal for premature babies to have stomach issues. My mother said she did not believe it was just a new stomach problem. She said it was the violent vomiting that made her doubt it was a premature stomach at play here.

I was born around eight pounds, and by the fifth week of life I had lost three pounds. One of the doctors called me pigeon because I had become so small. A more accurate examination concluded that I was born with a condition called Pyloric Stenosis.

At the age of five weeks old I had my first surgery. I was under full anesthesia for the first time. The surgery opened the blockage from the stomach to the intestine which then allowed the food to be absorbed. My health became a point of concern from the day I was born. I think it was the beginning of the underlying reason for my interest in health.

I don't know what the time frame was, but some time during my toddler stage and prior to the start of school I had my tongue clipped. That's what they called it. It was also called tongue tied. The doctor would knock you out and then cut the cord away from the tip of the tongue to allow more freedom of movement. People who have a lisp need to have this done to eliminate it.

That was my second time under full anesthesia. This procedure was very mild in comparison to the abdominal surgery. It did however require a hospital stay of a few days. This stay, from what I recall, was more of an opportunity for me to run wild and play with the other children on the floor. I really wasn't sick; it was a very simple surgery that did not require much recuperation time. I would get out of bed in the morning and play to my heart's content. Until the morning I woke up and found myself in a cage.

I remember the night prior a nurse came in my room, pulled my pajamas down and shot me up with a dull needle, loaded with a drug that knocked me out. Nice, huh? They had put me in a hospital bed that had iron bars on the sides, and the top had a steel and plastic dome. The reasoning behind the confinement was so I could heal, but I knew it was because I was too full of energy for the nurses.

I remember my mother came to visit me. I asked her to get me out, but the nurses would not let her. I was trapped in that thing for others convenience. They kept me in that hospital bed cage like an animal to force me to stay still. I think being in an incubator caused me to be claustrophobic. I felt very uncomfortable in that cage. I mean hospital bed.

It was around the age of four years old that my parents seemed to have trouble containing the energy that came with being me. I'm not sure why I was full of energy most of the time. I wondered if my parents expected me to be like my sisters, or what it was that I was doing wrong. I have fun operating at the peak of my energy.

The fact that I was a capable child, led my parents to place me in kindergarten at the age of five years old. The age of five was an acceptable age in those days for a child to begin school. In my case however, I turned five in the last week of August and began school the first week of September. I made the legal requirement by a few days. The thinking was I would be well served having school to focus on. The school work was the first attempt to occupy my mind with the important things in life.

My oldest sister is three years older than me. The next to the oldest sister is two years older than me. It wasn't as if school was not known to me. I did of course see my sisters leave the house for school for years. My father would leave for work, my sisters would leave for school, and once they were gone the house became calm. The hectic energy would drop off. My younger sister is four years younger than me. This gave me, a couple of years when the house was, just me and my mother for a few hours during the school days.

I felt a sense of peace when it was just the two of us. My mother always seemed to either understand me better than others did, or let me be freer. She would do her thing and I would have the house to myself without my sisters butting in. My mother and I sometimes would go out to lunch and just be together just the two of us. The unfortunate aspect of our relationship was that she would cave into others' way of handling me. I believe against her instincts, although maybe that was just my belief.

The few years of our private mornings, unfortunately did come to an end. My time to start school came too quickly for me. My mother took me to the place that sold the school uniforms. Kimball's clothing store on Main Street. Kimball's had the navy blue pants, the light blue shirts, and the ugly red ties that were required by the school. Kimball's also carried shoes. This was the first time I ever was measured for clothes. It was kind of weird, the old man measured me from head to toe then he handed me these very long pants to put on. It was the first time I used a dressing room. The pants were longer than my feet, so the guy had me stand on a round little table while he made the pants shorter. If he measured my legs, than why did he give me the long pants?

He kept pulling at my pant leg and saying something to my mother about a cuff and a hem. It all seemed unusual to me. I normally get pants that fit, why don't you just go get a pair that fits? This place is full of clothes and you have to alter these? I don't understand, but hey my mother seems ok about it so what do I care.

He told my mother the clothes would be ready for me in a few days, so we left. I remember thinking, when those clothes are ready I will be that much closer to starting school.

The night before school, I remember being nervous and wondering what it was that the morning would bring. My new school uniform was cleaned and pressed, my new school shoes were polished, and all I needed to do was go to sleep and let tomorrow come.

The morning came abruptly with the same rush of my sisters and my father trying to get ready to go. The difference this morning was that I had been added to the mix. My mother was getting dressed to bring me in to school for my first day. I knew what to do, but felt as though I was lost in the shuffle.

I remember getting dressed in my school clothes as if they were some magical type of garments that signified an important event. I ate my breakfast, brushed my teeth and down the long set of steps to the car I went. I got in the car with my sisters and mother and off we went.

The ride seems of great importance to me, and yet my sisters are unaffected. My mother gets us here on time and my sisters run off. My mother comes around to the side of the car, takes my hand and we walk down the driveway. On the right she explains is the convent. This is where the sisters live. The people who teach at this school are all sisters.

This is a Catholic school and I will study religion along with the other required courses. I know this is a Catholic school, because my sisters and I are required to wear uniforms to school.

We also go to church on Sundays. We go to the 10:30 mass almost every Sunday. It is just another place where we have to be quiet.

As we reach the front door I sense seriousness coming from my mother. This is a side of her I have not seen. This is different from a doctor's visit, less concern, more respect. As she is reaching for the door, a simple smile comes to her face. I take the smile as comfort; she is probably smiling because now all three kids are out of the house.

We walk down a short corridor that has a set of stairs to the left and a brown wooden door straight ahead of us. We continue down the hall and take a left just as it ends. She stops, let's go of my hand and says, "this is it, this is your room."

The feeling of abandonment and uncertainty is washing over me. I knew this was going to happen; I might as well suck it up and go in.

The energy I feel coming from this room at this moment, to me, is chaos. I'm able to see and feel the energy coming from the children in the room.

I can see and feel the spirits of the family members who are with these kids in spirit. I can feel the collective energy of lives being lived coming at me, with no way to stop it, or understand it.

Whenever I am receiving information, I am placed in a highly receptive state. This state causes such an intense peak of brain function that I cannot break from it. Now, this is happening to me on the first day of school!!! This is happening to a five year old child.

There are children crying, laughing, and a woman dressed in a black dress, with a strange white and black nurse's hat on. The woman is Sister Mary something and she wants everyone to know that she is in charge. She meets me at the door as I am saying goodbye to my mother. I am saying goodbye to the daily bits of peace and acceptance that have been the past two years.

I am being lead into this cinder block and wood room filled with strangers. A room with walls made of cinder blocks and painted an unpleasant color green. A room with windows along one side, that no one is to look out of. A room that has a big black board at one end of it. A room that has a big desk in front of a number of smaller desks aligned in rows, facing the big desk.

The desks have children sitting at them. How do they know to sit at that particular desk? What am I supposed to do? What is going on here? I've lost my sense of peace. Where did my mother go? Who are these kids? What is it I am hearing? This room seems louder than it actually is.

Sister Mary someone tells me where to sit. As I sit here it is overwhelming to me to be in a room that is so over run with such emotion. The energy seems to be everywhere. I can feel all the sadness, excitement, fear, and loneliness that are in this room. I can feel the nun walking around the room with an air of sympathy and self satisfaction. I can't understand why the room seems so loud and full of people when in fact, I'm looking around at mostly quiet children, sitting at their desks.

I don't know why, but I can feel Sister Mary what's her name and she does not like me. I know this sounds typical of a child to say, but she looks at me, as if she knows there is something going on with me. What that something may be makes her uncomfortable.

I sit at my desk taking in all that is in the room. The girl, who can't stop crying all day, keeps getting my attention. The kids, who seem so relaxed and comfortable in this room with me, seem even more out of place.

The wall switches have chrome cover plates and black switches. There's a flag on the wall. There are books all over the place.

The chairs are hard and cold with an odd shape to the seat. They are very uncomfortable and we have to stay in these all day! There is a clock on the wall. There's a crucifix on the wall. There is a picture of Mary on the wall.

There is a thing called the cloak room. I call it a closet. So much change. There are instructions and things to do. I wonder where my mother is, and what she might be doing. I know my sisters are in the building, but I have no idea where. Whew, they're here so it must be ok.

How long have I been sitting here? I need to get up and walk around. I can't just sit here. Oh, I can't get up until I am told I can.

We all go to the bathroom at the same time? Did she just say we all go to the bathroom at the same time? There is only one bathroom in my house and there are only six of us. ALL of us will go together, when is that? I need to do something other than sit here. How long have I been sitting here? Ten minutes!

She just keeps talking. Look at the shape of that kids head; my God he has a big head. Everyone is looking at a book. Where's my book? What are we doing? Work? It's the first day; I don't want to do this. Am I the only one who can think of better things to do? Let's go back to the instructions.

What are we doing? I'm so lost. When did she say anything about the book? Where was I? My God the room is so quiet now. Everyone is still here, how did it become so quiet? Ok I guess I better catch up.

After a short period of work it's time to go to the bathroom. Finally, I need to get up and walk around. As soon as it is time to line up for the bathroom, a surge of energy comes over me.

We all seem to need to do something. I get in line, ready to experience the great bathroom adventure we have heard so much about.

Yes! I'm not at my desk, we get to go somewhere and do something. I wonder if I will see one of my sisters, I hope one sees me. What did she say we have to be quiet? We have to be quiet away from our desk? When do we get to talk and make noise? Well, going to the bathroom doesn't seem to be as much fun as I had hoped it would be.

She leads us down the hall to two big wooden doors. Girls on one side, boys on the other, that's what I keep hearing. Stand here, three at a time, what does that mean? Three at a time, boys on this side and girls on that side. These people have rules for everything. I thought going to the bathroom was going to be fun. Wait my turn? I don't have to go to the bathroom.

I walk into this room that has white, long sinks on the wall and boys are peeing into them!! I look past the long sinks and see regular sinks. Across from the long sinks are three gray steel doors with toilets in them.

This place smells funny, kind of sweet and soapy. I remember seeing the other boys all peeing into the long sinks so I go over to one of them, and to my surprise I do have to pee.

I feel like I am going to get in trouble for peeing in this long sink. One of the boys just said the name of the long sinks, what did he call it, a urinal? That's what the pee sink is a urinal? What is Sister Mary someone doing in here, telling us to wash our hands and get back in line? Wow, no girls are supposed to be in the boy's room.

She never stops telling us what to do, and to be quiet. I'm in the bathroom and I'm told to be quiet? This is not fun. Now I have to get back in line and I can't talk to anyone?

The kid in front of me smells different. These walls are cold. Hey, the girls take longer than the boys, and we have to stand here and wait for them, and be quiet?

Who just touched me? I think the kid behind me just touched me. I turn around to look at him, and he is standing there with kind of a goofy smile, as if he did it on purpose.

What did she say? She's telling someone to turn their eyes front? What does turn your eyes front mean? It seems to be getting louder. Why is this kid now nodding his goofy head at me and laughing?

Oh, me? You want me to turn and keep my eyes front? This kid touched me and I … What, quiet and don't talk? I was just saying that I felt him touch me, so I turned around to see if he realized it. Now your yelling at me to keep my eyes front, aren't they in front by nature? I don't understand what that means.

First there is a cloak room instead of a closet. Next there is a long pee sink they call a urinal. Now I have to keep my eyes front! My eyes are always in front, that's where they belong.

The girls are done so back to the class room. I have no more enthusiasm in me in regards to the bathroom experience. Look at the shape of that kids head, I forgot about him. How is it that the girls are so quiet? Why do they take so long? Boy these walls are pretty smooth for cement. I think the goofy kid just touched me again; maybe he just can't walk very well.

The doors open and the other kids are going in, where is my desk?

There is a feeling again of restlessness in the room. The teacher is saying, "Settle down". Settle down? What does that mean? "Children take you seats", and do what with them? I just don't get her. There goes the crying girl again. She just keeps crying. Oh, there's the goofy kid, he seems like he's laughing all the time. Why doesn't she say something to him? This place smells funny.

Oh look the sun is out; I bet the dog is glad it's not raining out. When it rains and the dog gets wet, she smells bad. My mother makes sure we bring the dog in before she gets wet, or sometimes, she scratches at the door so we let her in. She sheds a lot. She is part Collie and part German shepherd. Her name is Ginger, she's a nice dog.

What are we doing now? What did I miss? Take out your pencils. I'm beginning to think there will never be any fun at school.

I wish that the man, standing beside the crying girl, would make her stop crying. He looks over at me sometimes, like I can do something about her crying. The teacher tries to ignore her, but it's not helping.

How do these classmates of mine know what to do? They seem so calm and accepting of this teacher, I don't get it. Why does she seem to talk to just them at times? Have they been here at school before?

I want to go home. I want to go back to having a peaceful morning. I want to go see my dog. I'm hungry and want something to eat. There is so much quiet noise around me, I don't like it. I want this all to stop!!!

The crying girl still has that same man standing beside her. He knows I see him, because when he looks at me I look back at him. I want to say to him, "don't look at me, and shut her up." I know, no talking out loud.

He is a tall, thin man probably around seventy years old. He must be her grandfather. I know he is trying to help her, but I wonder if he is scaring her or making her sad. He is well groomed, wearing a dark gray suit with a white shirt and a thin tie. I wonder when he died, he seems upset that she is so upset.

His attempts to comfort her are not working. I am aware of all that is going on in the room, how is this less important than all these rules? Which adult am I to listen to? I sometimes see an older gray haired woman on the right of the room as well.

She just kind of comes and goes. I wonder who she is. She is kind of fat; you know the round grandmother type. She's wearing a nice flowered skirt with a blouse and sweater. She seems like a nice woman. I don't know, if she knows, I can see her.

The older man that is on the crying girls left side seems unsure what to do. When he looks over at me, he kind of smiles. I think he's happy to know I see him. He doesn't scare me when he looks at me.

What did she say? What are we doing now? There's too much going on in here. This place hurts my head.......

4 Harrison Ave.
The Place I call Home

Chapter 2

T he bus pulls up in front of 4 Harrison Ave., the door opens and I wait as my sisters exit the bus. We all know its girls first. I'm the youngest, so I have to let them go first. As I wait, I feel the bus idling, under my feet. I can smell the diesel fuel exhaust coming in the open door.

I can't wait to take these school clothes off. I can't wait to be away from all this unfamiliar energy, it's not where I want to be. Finally, it's my turn to get off the bus; it always feels like an eternity getting off this bus. Wow, that last step is really high off the ground!

Eleven steps to go to get to the door. There's some sand on the first couple of steps, that's because the cars go by and blow sand on them. There are a couple of steps with cracks on them. Half way up, one of the steps has a piece broken off. It has a triangle shaped hole on it, when I get to this step; I know I'm half way to the door.

Just a few more stairs then a landing, then two more steps and home at last, another school day down. I know this place can be a little crazy at times, but at least there is something to eat. My mother usually has a good snack for us when we get home. One of my favorite snacks is the saltine crackers with chocolate frosting in the middle. I'm always hungry! I don't know how she knows, but my mother always knows when I need to eat.

After I have my snack, I'll change into my play clothes and go play in the yard, unless my mother won't let me eat in my school clothes. I wonder who came up with these uniforms anyway. A light blue shirt, red tie and navy blue pants, seems kind of odd to me. I get the shirts dirty real fast. I guess I spill stuff sometimes. The navy blue pants don't seem to get dirty as fast as the shirts. They rip easy.

My mother has to sew the rip or iron on patches. She and my father get mad when I tear my pants. I play too hard at recess they tell me. It seems I always fall on my knees and that's the most common tear to my pants. I even rip through the patches sometimes. When I tear the patches in my knees, a lot of times the next day, wow, does my mother get mad. I know when she is really mad at me, she uses my full name. Today she wants me to change my clothes before I can have my snack.

Up the stairs I go to my bedroom. I place my shirt on the hanger in the closet, just like they tell me to. I have to take my pants off and put them in the drawer. My parents want me to hold my pants upside down and put the seams together. The pants then have to be put, cuff first, into the top drawer. This way the drawer holds the pants, once it's closed. The pants hang outside the drawer. This is how I keep my pants looking like they are pressed. I always knock them down though, when I get to close to the dresser.

Oh well, play clothes on, its snack time! Today its cake, down to the kitchen I go. The kitchen is at the back of the house with a bathroom off of it. It's the only bathroom we have. The bathroom is not the place to be when the whole family is at the kitchen table. Let's just say that everyone knows where you are and everyone is pretty sure what you're doing.

I eat my snack and drink my milk, at the table with my mom and my sisters. Mmm, I can feel the cold milk slide down to my stomach. I'm full now but it won't last too long. I have to wait until my mother says I can go out and play. She likes to talk with us about school and our day. You want to know about my day?

I waited all day to come home, eat and go outside! There, that was my day. "Can I go outside now?"

I like being in the yard. Nobody bothers me in the yard. You know like the kind of stuff that happens in school, like the crying

girl's visitor. I can feel I'm being watched from the windows sometimes, but they stay inside. They must not be allowed to come outside. It must stink to have to stay inside all the time. The people I
sometimes see in the windows seem sad. I wonder why they're so
sad. I'd be sad if I was stuck inside all the time.

Did I tell you that when I see these things, I hear someone talking
to me? You know what I mean? I hear what the people I see want me
to hear, but at the same time, there is a voice that guides me through
the event. The voice I hear is mine but it's older. When this voice or
guidance is with me, I feel comforted and I'm able to stay calm and
listen.

Oh, the dog needs water; I'd better give her some. She drinks a
lot of water. She must spill it while I'm at school. That's one of my
jobs. I have to feed the dog and make sure she has water.

I play all kinds of games in the yard. I play football, I run around
playing with the dog, some days I practice being an actor. I think the
reason I think about acting so much is because I always feel like I'm
being watched.

They tell us in school that God is always watching; maybe that's
part of it too. I know my mother watches me play in the yard when
she is in the kitchen.

Today I feel like running around for awhile. I'm going to run up
and down the hill and jump over the wall in the yard and pretend I'm
an army man. Playing an army man is fun, because I pretend that I
get shot sometimes and just fall on the ground, like I'm dead.

I know I'll run down the hill and at the bottom, I'll pretend I get shot and just fall down. Just before I get to the bottom, bang, I'm shot. I can feel myself falling in a very violent way. I know I won't get hurt because the grass is soft. I let the force of the fall take me. As I tumble and twist to the ground, I think, this is a perfect time to practice being an actor.

I let the force of the fall do whatever it will, which means pushing my feet and arms in a crazy position as I hit the ground. My clothes get rearranged on my body.

I lay here holding my breath. I know a real actor does his own stunts, and I need to practice being real. I hold my breath and don't move so the look of being dead will leave no doubt in the director's mind.

I'm wearing a red t-shirt and during the fall, it rolled up to my neck.

What I don't know is that my mother happened to look out the window at the beginning of the fall. From the window in the kitchen, all my mother can see is her eight year old son take a nasty fall. He is now lying on the ground motionless, not breathing and probably bleeding severely from the neck!!!

She comes running out of the house toward me, screaming, Jeffrey!!! She gets about five steps out the door, when I pop up and say, "I was just playing", Ha ha ha,. The look on her face is diminishing panic that is being replaced with a look of, you jerk...

I ask her," Why are you yelling?" As she catches her breath, she says, "I saw you fall and from the angle I was at, it looked to me that you had blood coming out of your neck. You weren't breathing for a long time. I have to admit; I smile as I think what a great job of acting. I fooled my own mother.

I better just roll down the hill for the rest of today. I like rolling down the hill. This is what you have to do. You have to hold on to the wire fence at the top of the hill, so you can lie down. Once you're all laid out, you just let go.

It's fun because after a few times you get dizzy, if you get too dizzy though you can get a headache. The other thing about rolling down the hill is that, I always know when winter is coming.

The colder the weather becomes the harder the ground gets. Once the ground starts to get hard, a few times down the hill and it starts to hurt. The other bad thing about late fall and winter is, I have to go in the house when it's dark.

If I don't have any home work, I get to play in the basement. The basement can be fun when you're with someone, but when you're alone it can be a lit-tle scary! If I don't want to play in the basement, I watch F Troop and Lost in Space on TV, in the den, while waiting for my father to get home.

I always know when he's home, because he throws his keys on the wooden desk near the front door, and it's loud. If you did something wrong during the day, my mother will tell my father. Then he either talks to us, or spanks us, depending on the nature of the offense.

Yeah, the key noise can either signal joy or sorrow depending on how your day went. A lot of times for me, it was right in the middle.

Most days he comes in, throws the keys down and sits in the kitchen reading the news paper while my mother makes dinner.

We all eat together, but there's not a lot of conversation. Once we're done, my sisters have to clear the table, wash, dry and put away the dishes. I have to do the dishes sometimes too, but not as often as they do. When I wash the dishes, my clothes always get wet, so I'm told to dry. Drying the dishes is so boring to me. No fun involved in rubbing a plate with a cloth. When I wash, at least I can slosh the water around and play with the suds... I guess that's why I have to dry.

Once the kitchen is clean and everything is put away, it's back to the desk to finish our homework, I hate homework. Can't they just teach at school?

My father built us this desk in the dining room, so we all have a place to do our homework. It's a big desk that has space for two chairs and it has two long shelves above the desk. It also has a set of four drawers to the right of each chair.

The four of us kids were all given a drawer of our own. This is where we keep our papers, pens and small things. My drawer is the bottom drawer on the left side. Obviously, I didn't choose the drawer; my father told us who would get which one.

One day I pulled the drawer too far, and it came all the way out! I found there is a space under the drawer. Hey, I can put stuff here and even if the drawer is open it won't be seen. Pretty cool, huh?

The two long shelves are loaded with books. There's an entire encyclopedia set on one shelf with a big blue dictionary, and a bible. The other shelf has all my mother's books on it.

The book I need the most is the big blue dictionary. I use the dictionary the most, because my spelling is not very good. If I ask my father how to spell a word he always says, "Look it up." How do you expect me to look up a word that I can't spell? If I can't spell it, how do I find it? So frustrating!

My constant use of the dictionary did turn out to be a good thing. I was looking up yet another word one day when I found myself in the E section of the dictionary. As I read down the page I saw, ESP. I know I've heard of ESP before, but I don't know exactly what it is. As I read the words, I hear them coming off the page and into my head with such clarity, I feel as though they are being read to me. As I read the definition again, I'm relieved to know there is an explanation for what I experience.

ESP, is defined as an ability to communicate with non physical means. (Webster's dictionary) Wow, that's what happens to me! That explains it! Wow, wow, wow! I have to tell somebody! I have to do something. I pull out my drawer and with the big black marker, I write, Jeff's ESP on the outer end of my drawer. I have to let this out. I have to let someone know I understand now!

While I'm sitting on the floor in front of my drawer, and with the dictionary still beside me, my little sister comes over to the desk. She opens her drawer; she has the bottom drawer on the other side. She's just looking at me funny as I tell her what I've learned. That's ok; she's too young to understand, it will be our secret. Huh, this has to be MY secret ESP, extrasensory perception, fits what I experience. All this time the doctors and teachers have been telling me and my parents that I'm hyper active. I'm not hyper active. I have ESP!

The high energy I experience, and the sleepless nights are being caused by ESP, not being hyper active. The doctors and teachers have convinced my parents that I need Ritalin. How do I tell the grownups in my life that I have figured it out? That they are wrong? How does a child explain to the adults who are always frustrated with you, that there is nothing that I can do?

Oh yeah, I was telling you about the house. I mentioned the basement being scary at times, right? There is an oil barrel at the bottom right side of the stairs as you go down. These are the stairs that go from the dining room to the basement. When you walk by the oil barrel to go back up the stairs, you can see and feel a man come from behind the oil barrel, and try to grab you. Yes, that's what I said. See, and feel the man come from behind the right side of the barrel and grab at you with his left hand. He never comes out from behind the barrel, and he always has the same expression on his face.

He's a skinny man that is about fifty years old. His hair is mostly gray. He's dressed in these old looking work clothes. He always has the same light gray shirt on and dark gray pants. His face is dirty looking. His face is shaped like a triangle. If I get too close, I feel him even more, so I always run by the oil barrel. I'm not the only one that sees him either. My sisters see him too.

He's creepy! Once I make it passed the oil barrel and run up the stairs, I'm back in the dining room; you know where the desk is.

To get to the second floor, I have to either walk through the hall or go through the living room.

We're not supposed to go in the living room because that's for special occasions. You know Christmas and when we have company over. So, I go through the living room to go up stairs, ha, ha ha. I always, listen for those keys...

The second floor has our three bedrooms there. The front room of the house is where my parents sleep. When I have a bad dream, I go in and wake up my mother. She lets me climb in bed between her and my father. Many times when I lay there unable to sleep, a clown made of light, appears on top of the bedroom door. I know your saying, WHAT?

The door opens to the right and stops against the wall. The open door allows light from a night light that is in the hallway, to cast a sliver of light on the top portion of the open door. The light turns into a dancing clown, once my parents fall asleep. It will wave to me if I wave to it. It dances and entertains me while I lay there trying to sleep. This happens a lot. It happens to my sisters too. We see the dancing clown, who waves to us and tries to bring us comfort. I told you it can be crazy at times, didn't I?

Across the hall there is another bedroom that has a full length mirror attached to a door that leads to a storage room. There are times when I'm standing in front of the mirror, I see people looking back at me. These people are all around the edge of the mirror, one head on top of another, not in the center. It seems like they are just curious about what is going on. It's as if the clown and the people in the mirror are there to participate in the moment, not to cause harm in anyway. The guy behind the oil barrel though, who knows what he wants.

The bedroom that I slept in is on the opposite side of the room with the mirror. It's an average size room with one closet in it. The house is a Cape, so that means I have a big sloping ceiling on one side of the room, this slope is where I hang my posters sometimes.

There's also a picture of St. Jude on the wall. He's the patron saint of hopeless causes. I wonder who put that in my room?

I have a twin size bed, a side table with a crucifix on it and one dresser for my clothes. There's only one window in my room, and it faces the back yard.

My bedroom is over the den, so when I go to bed at night, I can hear the TV down stairs. It doesn't bother me to hear it; it actually helps me sleep at times.

I often have trouble sleeping because my room can be a very busy place. It's as if, I can never be alone. I either have my family around me or these people around me. I call them people even though they are spirits. They seem to want to tell me things. Most times they are all talking at once and I can't understand a single word that is being said. I have grown accustom to using this time to sleep.

I wonder why they want to be with me. I wonder why they interrupt my peace. Sometimes I see them in my bedroom window when I'm outside playing. I feel like they want my help, but I don't know what to do for them. Maybe I should give them my Ritalin, it does nothing for me.

I like when the window is open during the summer because I can hear the cars go by and as it gets later, I can hear the crickets. The crickets get so loud at times it's like their in my room.

The first floor is not an active place to me, although there are several times when the dining room table shakes as if someone walked into it.

The way the house was constructed has been changed over the years. The kitchen has a set of steps outside, that lead to a window that once was a door.

I often think that the people who are walking through the house are walking around as if it were in the condition the house was in many years ago.

So remember, inside the house you've got the creep in the basement, the mirror that seems to go to another world, the dancing clown, and people in my room at night, and the banging dining room table.

From the outside, I can see people looking out the windows at me. The second floor front window always has someone looking out it. I can see the curtain move at times when I come home and I know there is no one in the room. I said at the beginning of this chapter, it gets a little crazy at times but its home. It is the home I live in.

Meet the Family

Chapter 3

Top Left: John and Pat
Mary (aunt) James & Madelaine McBride
Top Right: Doris Kearns
Middle: Jack McBride, Patricia Kearns
Bottom: Jane, left. Lisa, Kerry McBride

I guess this is as good a time as any to introduce you to the family. I come from a predominately Irish catholic family. I could trace my father's side of the family back to 1860. William and Mary

McBride were my great grandparents. I only know they were born in Massachusetts some one hundred and fifty years ago. I don't know what they did for work. I do know they had four children, one of whom was my grandfather, James McBride who was born in 1892.

James McBride married Madeline O'Sullivan, who was also born in 1892. These two turn of the century kids spent over thirty years married. Madeline was a stay at home mom.

James was an educated man who was a business owner and a licensed master plumber. He was later the town plumbing inspector. He was a nice man, who I spent a lot of time with, their marriage produced four children.

Their youngest boy John, or Jackie as he was called, was my father. Jack was born in 1932. John spent time in the air force during the Korean War and later became employed by what is now AT&T. He was an intelligent, hard working man, just as the other men in his family were. He taught me how to use tools and how to fix just about anything.

John met Patricia Kearns in high school. Pat was born in 1934 the daughter of Doris and Austin Kearns. Jack and Pat married in 1954 and had four children of their own, three girls and one boy. I am that boy.

I never met my mother's father Austin. From what I was told he left my grandmother when my mother and her brother Brian were young kids. My mom stayed at home with us until we were in our teens. She then worked as a secretary for a local company.

My mother's side of the family is, I believe, the source of most of the umm, visitors, that I have. I'll try to explain.

The family tree on my mother's side goes back to my great-great grandparents. I hope I don't lose you.

My grandmother was born in 1914 in Fitchburg, Mass. Her parents were born in the late 1890's, in Salem Ma. Edwin and Alice Whipple were their names.

Alice's mother, Cora Parsons, was born in Salem Ma., in the mid 1800's. She was the daughter of Walter Whipple who was also born in Salem Ma. My guess is in the late 1700's.

There were multiple generations of family members, who originated in Salem, Massachusetts on my mother's side.

They were all from my grandmother's family. As for my grandfather Austin Kearns, all I know is that his father's name was Thomas Kearns. I think they were from Adams, Massachusetts.

Whenever the conversation came around to my mother's family being from Salem, Ma. The topic of interest was that a distant female family member of the Parson's, was hung during the Salem witch trials.

I don't have any confirmation as to what exactly happened, other than the woman's name was Mary Parson's and she would have been a great-great aunt to me. Mary is Cora's sister. Cora is my great-great grandmother.

I wish I could give you a little more on this subject, but you now know about as much as I do.

So thanks for meeting the family, I tried to keep it short.

The Great Escape

Chapter 4

I have trouble with my knees, remember the school pants? When I walk, sometimes my legs just give out. Like when I'm out at recess, my legs just kind of buckle and I fall on my knees. My doctor told my mother it's because, I'm growing too fast. Huh? I don't think I'm growing fast enough. How can you grow to fast anyway? Doesn't the body know what it's doing?

He tells my mother I need to go to another type of doctor. He called him an orthopedic. He's a bone doctor they tell me. I guess he knows about knees too.

A few weeks later I have an appointment with the new doctor. I notice as soon as we walk in the door that this guy isn't like my other doctor. His waiting room has no small chairs, no toys, no coloring books and it defiantly doesn't smell like my doctor's office. I don't think he has many kids as patients.

I wonder if I have to get a shot. It's so quiet in here. How long do I have to sit here anyway? My mother tells me to read something; yeah, I just left school, no thanks. Then just sit there she says. "Hhmm" aggravating.

The nurse opens the door and calls my name, finally! As we walk to the door, I can feel myself get nervous, I wonder if I have to get a shot. The nurse seems nice; I don't feel like she'll be giving me a shot. - No- nope, no sense of having to get a shot today, good! Whew, it's times like these that I'm glad I know things.

Just like all my other doctors visits, the nurse brings me to a small room. I have to get undressed and sit on the table with the paper on it. It's fun for me to move around and have the paper make noise.

This room has funny looking stuff in it. There are pictures of bones on the walls and fake skeletons on the shelves. There are these littler triangular hammers on a silver tray, and a lot of ace bandages. My mother says the bandages are for casts. "Casts? I ask her, "Am I going to get a cast?" She laughs and I say, "Don't laugh, how do I know. I go to the doctor's all the time and they do things to me."

The doctor comes in the room and the first thing I notice is he's tall. That explains why there are no small chairs in the waiting room. He seems nice though. He tells me to sit up and hang my legs off the side of the table. Well, so far so good, no bad feeling from this guy.

He holds my right thigh against the table and moves my knee around in a circle. "Hmm" he says. He does the same thing with my left leg and he says, "hmm" again. I think, " hmm," that's it? He stands there for a moment than turns to my mother and tells her my knees are loose. "Hey! Hello", I knew that before we went to the first doctor.

He tells me to stay put and asks my mother for her pocket book. She gives him her pocket book and he puts the strap over my foot. Ok, this is weird. He tells me to lift my foot straight out and to keep the pocket book on my foot.

I feel kind of funny using her pocket book because I'm not supposed to touch her purse. He wants me to do this ten times on each leg. He explains how this movement will make my knees stronger. He tells me to do this a few times per week and as my knees get stronger to put some books or something in the pocket book to make it heavier. I just look at my mother, knowing I won't be using her pocket book as my own.

Three days a week I sit on the edge of the kitchen table and do the exercise just like the doctor to told me to. It's funny to be sitting on the kitchen table, when I'm not even allowed to put my elbows on the table when I eat. I guess my parents think its ok for me to sit on the table to make my knees stronger, if it saves my school pants.

I like doing the exercise because it makes my knees feel better. I have to pay attention when I do this so the pocket book doesn't slip off my foot. It's fun having to think and to move a certain way at the same time. I look forward to the days that I do my exercises.

I use an old pocket book that my mother doesn't want anymore. I 'm now up to two books and a few bricks. My legs are starting to buckle a lot less. I can see my legs are getting bigger too. I guess this doctor knows what he's talking about.

The bad thing is my legs make the rest of my body look even scrawnier than before. I want to do some weight lifting for the rest of me. I know my muscles grow fast because of my legs. I need to find a way to build my upper body now too.

I've seen barbells before, but I don't know where I can get some. I think I'll see what I can find in the basement to use as weights. There are all kinds of stuff on shelves down there, I'll find something. Yup, down the stairs, past the creep behind the oil barrel, I go.

My father keeps scrap pieces of wood and other things all over the basement. He lets me make stuff out of these scraps when he's finished with his work. The first thing I need is a pole. I know he has an old broom stick somewhere up in the ceiling over his work bench. If it's still there, I can use it for my bar. I climb up on his bench and there it is an old broom stick on top of some boards. It's covered in thick dust, so I guess he doesn't need it.

Now, I need to get some weight for the ends of the stick. There is a shelf across from his bench with old pots and pans on it. I know I'll nail an empty pan to each end of the stick. The pans can hold the weight. I see two matching pans way in the back of the shelf. Perfect, I'll just nail the handles to the stick.

Have you ever tried to nail metal pans to a wooden broom stick? It's a lot harder than I thought. After about an hour of bending nails and fighting with the stick, I have my barbell ready! It should be perfect because the pans stay flat on the floor and the stick is off the ground, just like real weights.

Now that I have my barbell all I need is weight. There is sand in a hole in the floor. I know, I'll fill the pans with sand and that will be my weight! I grab a plastic beach shovel and fill the pans almost to the top. They aren't very big; I think these are called sauce pans. Anyway, I have my barbell, now it's time to use it.

The first exercise I want to do is for my arms. So I'll pick up the stick, and lift it up with my arms. Half way up and the sand spills all over the floor.

Opps, that's ok I'll just put the sand back in the pans and try again. Ok, all the sand is back in the pans and as I lift it again, it doesn't work. One roll of the wrist and the sand is back on the floor, again. Hmm. This is not going to work, what a waste of my time this is. I hope it was ok to use those pans. I'd better just take the nails out and put them back. Sigh.

We have a swing in the back yard that's close to our neighbor's house. While I'm sitting on the swing, bored, the father comes out in his yard. He is a really nice guy, we always talk. I tell him about my sand and stick story and he says, "My sons left behind a small barbell set, you can have it if you want it." "YES! I'll take it. I'll take it right now." He says, "Meet me at my basement when you see the door open." "OK! I'm going right over to the basement door now." I can't wait to get these weights home. What timing!

As soon as he opens the door I see them piled up on the floor. "There they are, take them." He says. I load all the weights on the bar and head across the yard to the back door of my house. Wow, it's getting heavy, fast.

My father must have seen me coming because he's already at the back door. When he opens the door for me, I have to step back because the door opens out. As I step away from the door, one of the collars at the end of the bar falls off. Crash! The bar empties on the floor, one side, crash, and then the next. I know I'm in trouble that was really loud.

My father says, "This is going to be a long road." Well that wasn't so bad, I thought he was going to yell at me. I wonder what he means, a long road.

I start to reload the bar. My father says, "Hey", here it comes, and I know he has something to say. "Make two trips" he says.

Oh, that's a good idea; it's a long walk to the basement. Its eighty pounds, wow, these are my own actual weights! I'm so excited!

The basement has a couple of levels to it. The deepest part of the basement is where the furnace is. I'm going to put the weights there, so I can pick them up over my head without worrying about hitting the ceiling. I'm not that tall, but the basement is low in some spots. Plus by putting the weights near the furnace they will be warm.

I can start weight lifting today! I hope the rest of my body fills out like my legs do. I don't really know what I'm doing yet. I remember the doctor telling me to keep my bones still and lift with my muscles so that's what I'll do. I'll do every move my body makes with the weights in my hands.

The first thing I'm going to do is my arms! I pick up the bar and curl the weight to my chest. I do it ten times, just like my legs. That feels good; it's nice to have that warm feeling in my arms. It's even better not to have to cleanup sand. That was just dumb. I'm so glad I have these, I can't believe it.

I know from what the doctor told me, that I only need to exercise a few days per week so that's what I'll do. I won't just do my legs anymore I'll do as much of my body as I can. I really hope to balance out my body soon.

It's now been a couple of months of regular workouts. I'm beginning to see my body respond really well.

It's like magic to me to feel the change my body makes. The pumping up of the muscles and the release of energy is just the thing

I need. I have such a pure sense of freedom when I exercise. I can't hear anyone talking to me when I workout. The only thing I hear and feel is me. It's nice to get away from all that.

These past months I have found my body is more peaceful. My appetite is better and my sleep if far more restful. I wish I started sooner. My bad knees are to thank for my new peace. Just to be clear, the only escape is during the exercise itself. While I rest in between sets, I come right back to all the energy. It never leaves me.

Sometimes when I look out the little window in the basement, I see little kids looking in on me. It's strange because they are normally inside looking out. These are young children I see looking in and wondering what I'm doing. They aren't always there, just sometimes. They're dressed in old fashion clothes. They look in and if I go to the window they disappear. Unlike the man behind the oil barrel, I wish he would disappear.

I'm now on a mission to learn all I can about weight training. I'll talk with anyone who knows anything about weight lifting. I just love it.

I'm starting to learn about nutrition too. There is a small health food store in town. I go there on Saturday's and the lady, who works there, helps me. I'm amazed what vitamins and other products can do for my body. When I'm in the store, I have a sense of peace. I like the way it smells. I look at every bottle and thing in there. If she's busy, I just wonder around and I listen to the voice in me. I can reach for something and I'm told if I need it or not. It's the same voice I always hear. This voice is always with me. It seems to be an endless amount of information. This voice helps me so much. I'm glad to know it is there.

There is such peace and life in this store, I feel it. Sometimes I don't buy anything and I feel like she gets mad at me, but I don't always have money. I want to tell her I'll be back when I have some money, but I don't. I just leave.

I've also started doing odd jobs and part time work. Making a few dollars after school and on the weekends gives me enough money to start saving and to buy myself extra food and nutritional products. Eating just the food that is offered by my parents is not enough. I am always hungry, and yes I always say this. The food and vitamins that I buy really do help me feel better. I notice the better I feel, the higher the energy in me is. The better my energy is the more information I receive.

It's been about a year now that I have been using the weights in the basement. The basement workouts are going ok but, I need more equipment. So, I'm joining a weight lifting club with my friends. I know I'll learn more and they have a lot more stuff than I do.

They call it a club because it's a place for power lifters; they make only enough money to pay the bills. It costs me ten dollars a month because I'm a student. The gym is a few miles from my house and many times I walk to and from.

To get there I have to walk on Main Street. There is a book store on the corner about half way between the gym and home. I happen to look through the window one afternoon and I noticed there were weight lifting magazines on the shelf.

Being obsessed with weight training, I went in the store. I was surprised by the silence and at the amount of energy in the place. I can only describe it as the way I feel in a library. The information that is condensed in all the books feels like thick air to me. The weight lifting magazines section also has bodybuilding magazines. I've never seen these before.

I'm like wow, how cool, these guys have amazing bodies. I know right now, this is what I want to look like. I don't care about being strong. I just want to chase the pump. I want my body to look like these guys, only better. I know, today at the age of fifteen, what I'm going to do to my body. I know right here and now that I will be good at what it is these guys are doing. As I leave the store, I'm energized with a new direction and a sense of what is to come.

I returned to the weight lifting club ready to take my training in a new, exciting direction. Power lifters do fewer repetitions with heavy weight and take an extended break between lifts.

Bodybuilders do more repetitions with lighter weight and less rest in between sets. It's no surprise that I gravitated toward this type of training. It fits my pace of living like a glove.

The power lifting club members and I are as different as a high diver and a free style swimmer. We both use a pool but our goals are not the same. Seeing this club is designed for power lifters and I'm not a power lifter, I think I need to make some other arraignments.

The training is just about the only place I can go to escape the constant interference. So I've decided to get some equipment for the basement. I have a few thousand dollars in the bank and a need for peace.

A very helpful friend who owns a steel yard near my home has offered to help me make some equipment for the basement. He actually makes the equipment; I just wait for it to be completed. It is very generous of him to help me. While he makes the pieces, I order the weights and my father and I prepare the basement. Well my father prepares it, I just wait. Ha,ha, seems to be a pattern here.

I am so free and left alone when I workout. It is as though the energy it takes for me to receive information or intrusion is unable to function. I know it's still there but it seems to take a step back while I am engaged in physical work.

While some of the energy that's in me gets released, most of the energy intensifies and stays in my body. Like I said earlier it's magical, its relief.

I also see that my body doesn't just get a pump, my body expands. I grow rapidly, which I feel is a result of the energy that is stored in my body. The energy that is used to receive information seems to be transferred to a physical experience not just a mental state.

I'm starting to realize just how powerful this energy is. I'm starting to understand that I feel the emotions of others. I'm just starting to get a finger hold on just what it is that happens to me. I'm beginning to understand there is more to this than I thought there was.

The home gym is really starting to take shape. I have been able to make changes to the basement at will. My father let me cut his work bench in half and move it to a part of the basement it has never been in. We have cleared a large section of the basement and installed walls, electricity; lights and a mirror. Of course when I say we, I mean my father. I just wait...

The money I saved over the years is now flowing into this gym. I think it will be perfect for me.

Then a funny thing happened, a tractor trailer pulled up in front of our house with a very loud, Pcchhsss sound, as the driver put the brakes on. Equally as loud and without any doubt, the whole house in unison yells out, JEFFREY!! Ha ha ha, oops, I ordered another piece of equipment, didn't I tell you?

I run outside to meet with the driver who is looking at the hill that the house sits on and he says to me, "This is a tail gate delivery kid." "No problem, you get it off the truck and I'll do the rest." It's a hack squat unit. I'm so excited. My mother says "Where do you expect to put that?" I smile and say, "In the basement"; she just shakes her head and walks away. Crazy huh? Most sixteen year old kids want their driver's license. I just want a commercial quality gym in the basement of my parent's house, a place of peace and progress, to call my own.

It's Guidance Stupid!

Chapter 5

A s my junior year in High School starts, I enter my fifth year of football. Unfortunately, I have lost my drive for the sport. Today we had our third game, which we lost as usual. We spend five days a week and countless hours practicing, the same things over and over. We don't seem to be changing the way we do things. To me losing games on a regular basis should make it clear that we are doing something wrong, but I'm not the coach.

I stand on the practice field at times and wonder why I stay. The voice inside of me seems to be trying to get a message to me. Even though I'm one of the starters on the team, I don't like wasting my time, I don't like losing, and I don't like being injured. This is exactly what this feels like to me now, a waste of my time, energy and well being.

Football season starts in August and ends in November and by the end of this four month block of time I'm not as healthy as I was at the beginning of the season. I always prepare for the next season starting the day after the last one ends.

I can't work after school during the season so that means no income. No income means there's isn't any money for extra food.

I used to love the idea of being a big, strong, hard hitting football player. I've learned the big and strong part comes off the field; it comes from the weight room. As far as the hard hitting part is concerned, it's not as fulfilling or as long lasting as a great pump in the gym is to me.

I've been injured a few times while playing over these past years. I have a back injury right now that just won't go away. I have a heavy feeling I should stop playing. It's a feeling I can't shake. I know there is something better that I will be doing with this time. I feel I'm losing a piece of me by continuing to play.

So, regardless of what my friends and family might say to me, I'm done. I'm practicing hurt and I don't like this environment that I find myself in. So that's it, today is my last day. The voice deep inside me is getting stronger with every thought.

I start by turning in my equipment. I feel isolated with my decision to stop playing. First, I carry my helmet and pads from my locker to the equipment room. Then it's my uniforms, practice and game. Finally it's my spikes. That's everything the school owns. It's funny, I had to wait three years to get the best equipment available and today I return it in a matter of minutes.

I'm not sure if any of my team mates even realize what I'm doing. Next, I start stuffing all my things into my gym bag, soap, shampoo, socks, deodorant, t- shirts, everything.

I check my now empty locker, to make sure I have everything, wow, I'm doing this. I look around the locker room as everyone goes about their usual routine, they don't seem to notice I'm leaving. Should I say good bye? Ahh, I'll see them all in school on Monday, why bother.

I bend down and grab my heavy, over packed bag and slowly head toward the door. No more locker room for me, no more loud, smelly concrete building to report to as if I am a prisoner.

I have one last stop before the exit door, the coach's room. I stop at the closed door to compose myself. "You can do this, it's what you want, just open the door and let it begin." I say to myself. I place my bag to the left on the floor outside the door, why lug that in there, I think.

I stand at the door, and as I raise my right hand, I form a fist to knock. I hold my fist away from the door for what seems to be an eternity, and then I knock on the door, three times.

"Come in.", I hear. I take a deep breath as I reach down, turn the door knob and walk in the room.

The three coaches are sitting on chairs, as I enter the room. The assistant coach is in the back of the room to my right. The head coach is sitting on a chair in the center of the room and the line coach is closer to me, off to my left.

"What's up Mac?" the head coach asks. I take a deep breath and say, "I've turned my equipment in, and I'm done playing."

As I say this, I see the assistant coach's eyes widen and he smiles as he looks at me. I know he is getting a kick out of this, I feel he's not too crazy about this place as well. I watch as his eyes dart back and forth from the other coaches to me.

The head coach tries to talk me out of it, but I can feel he really could care less. I know he doesn't care too much about winning, why should he care about losing a player. His half hearted speech is nothing more to me than noise at this moment. I have already tuned you out buddy, so please save your speech.

I keep looking at the assistant coach who can't seem to stop smiling. He is saying so much to me without saying a word. Then the line coach starts telling me his ideas on my actions. He babbles on about walking away from adversity and some other nonsense about his life. How I should be strong and learn from his greatness.

Just as I'm thinking, you guys haven't won two games in a row in year, I hear that voice in me say; "You don't have to listen to this, just leave." So I turn, open the door and walk out. They don't understand what I feel and they have nothing to offer other than continued failure.

The heavy steel door closes behind me as I reach for my bag. I throw the bag over my shoulder and I open the exit door. As the door opens I feel the warmth of the sun on my face, as I take my first non football player's step in five years.

The further away I get from the football field, the better I feel about my decision. I'm glad I listened to my guidance and ended it. As I walk away from five years of football, I feel the road ahead of me is wide open. I feel free. I feel like I'm back.

I'm just not happy playing anymore. I miss my gym and I miss the workouts that bring me such peace. I know what it does for me, and I see what I will do with it. The excitement that comes with each workout is hard for people to relate to. I need something to over ride the constant mental connection to the other side that is with me. I need to express any energy that I can just to bring me to a place of peace.

I miss having a couple of bucks in my pocket. I feel like the weight of the world has been lifted off of me. I've reconnected to a part of me that normally got shut out during the season. That's over now.

My inner voice gave me the strength to follow through on my desire. The assistant coach gave me a sense of empowerment too. I guess you could say I used his energy.

The energy, as I call it, is now a constant. I know that it is in me, it's a tool that has been here for me for many years. I now have times when I call upon it as opposed to it calling on me.

I understand it a lot better now. Up until this point it seemed to be a sporadic, uncontrollable force. Like a tornado, you don't think about one until you see that funnel cloud coming. I believe the increase in my overall health is a big reason for this awareness.

I'm hearing things and seeing things in a way that no longer come to me without warning. I have a sense now of what the spike in my energy is all about. It's taken me all of these sixteen plus years, of life just to recognize when it's coming.

In the past the spike in energy, would happen just as an event was unfolding. This energy is what connects me to my guidance; it sends me into a much needed, higher sense of awareness.

I still have varying levels of incoming energy depending on the need, but it is less of a shock. I guess the best way to say it is I allow it to even out before I react now. I let the information become clearer. The leveling out of energy helps me to receive a broader view of all that is going on.

This is going to sound contradictory to you, but this is how it works. The more at peace I become, the more information I receive. The spike in energy is still there but it calms me to know help is on its way.

I realize I can feel other people more strongly now too. Just like the coaches, each one of them had a different response to me at that moment. I was aware of all of their thoughts while I was making my point.

By allowing the energy or information to expand, I gain a broader sense as to what I have available to me in that moment. I can focus on everything at once, my thoughts, their thoughts and incoming direction.

I'm getting better at knowing when an opportunity is presenting itself to me. Like being told to walk out the door, I knew there would be nothing that any of them would do.

I listen to my guidance, the guidance that helps me. I trust that voice within me more than anything else I know. It is the most powerful thing I have ever known.

I'm also learning that there are people who can sense what I do. Like Sister Mary what's her name, the kindergarten teacher. She has spent much of her life praying and studying the spiritual world. She is very much aware of the two worlds and what is involved in them. That's why most priests and nuns will say it was a calling that led them into their profession.

Now whether she knew exactly what it is I can do, I don't know. I do know that my energy levels, my sensitivity to the future and the connectivity to both worlds, make people uncomfortable.

Having the ability to know all this at a young age gives me a unique perspective. I have known there are two worlds that exist, all my life. I live in the physical world while staying connected to the spiritual world. Is it a good thing to know at this point in my life? I hope so.

I'm on my way home to tell my parents what I just did.

E.S.P. It's not as easy as it's spelled.

Nineteen months later!

Energy

Chapter 6

As I walk home from the football field I can't help but wonder how this day will end. I know what I did is right for me. My mother knows my back is pretty badly injured, so she'll be ok about it. My father? Well let's just say I'll be listening for those keys, once again…

I don't know about you, but it's really difficult for me to hide from myself. I realize compromise is important in life, but I need to know the energy I put into something is going to produce more than just regret.

Energy is life and in my case it takes a lot of it to keep all systems running. Obviously food and rest will create enough energy to maintain a normal functioning human being, but I require more.

To support the connection to the spiritual world, my never ending brain activity, and the physical activity in my day to day, I require a lot of calories. That's why I am always eating. If you have a healthy body, you have a healthy mind.

The energy or force within my body pushes me. I find it to be so strong at times it over rules all that is going on around me.

We all have that inner voice that guides us if we let it. My inner voice is always running its mouth. So when that voice wants to get its point across to me, it becomes inner voices. Not just one, but several voices. I also see spirits or people shaking their heads in a yes or no movement within my mind, they respond to the choice that I make.

I know your thinking this kid needs a shrink; he's hearing voices telling him what to do! It's not like that. I absolutely know its spiritual guidance, because it creates peace within my thought process.

When I walked out the door from football, I felt peaceful. The warm sun on my face, the release of the frustration from not doing what is right for me, brought me peace. This is what the force or inner voice creates, it brings peace.

It's not as though the thought of leaving the team just appeared in my mind and I walked off the field. I spent time considering all options and as I did this, the truth became clearer.

I wish I could explain this to my father as easily as I explained it to you. Somehow, I suspect it won't go as smoothly as it did with you.

Albert Einstein wrote that he believes humans need to speed up their mental energy to connect to the spirit world. He adds that the spiritual world needs to slow down to connect to us.

The increase in connectivity he refers to, I believe, is through meditation and prayer. His writing on the subject explains how he recognizes that the spiritual energy of the universe has to connect with our soul's energy. For this the frequency of both participants must be equal.

My experience has always been that I speed up when I connect to the stream of information that is going by. I only struggle to connect to existing energy in my life when I'm sick or injured.

I've mentioned repeatedly that it never leaves me. I'm glad it's there. I depend on this ability to know, to connect or whatever you want to call it.

John Lennon's song, "there's nothing you can know that can't be known, there's nothing you can see that can't be shown, there's nowhere you can be that isn't where you're supposed to be, it's easy, all you need is love…", Is a perfect example of what is available to us all.

The first time I heard the words in that song I understood what he was singing about. It seemed clear to me that other people can do what I do. They too can just stop and hear the stream of information that comes from God, or love, as he called it.

I mention this at this time because I know this is what is happening to me. E.S.P is only part of the bigger picture.

Yeah, heavy stuff for a teenager, but it is how I live. I know no other life, and I'm ok with that.

I know when I'm connected to the spiritual side of my life because my head has a hissing or a buzzing sound in it. This hissing sound is incoming energy. I wake up with it, I go to bed with it and it is active during my sleep.

I monitor my sleep for information that guides me. I also ask for answers to questions before I go to sleep. Many, many times I am given answers through dreams. These informative type dreams usually come prior to my waking up.

Now that the, "I quit the football team", energy has left the house, its back to my after school job and back to my regular workouts, AHHHH. Oh yeah and back to being able to take better care of myself.

Have I mentioned that I can see the future? Yeah, it's not just my every day contacts with spirits anymore. I now get flashes of small incidents like, I think of a song, and when I turn the radio on its playing. I think of someone I haven't seen in awhile and there they are at the store I'm in.

It's not the fact that I see the person or hear the song that is important to me. I want to know how I knew the song would be on. I want this process of knowing what's to come to be as constant as breathing.

We all have this happen to us. I am so aware of the mental process that makes this kind of stuff happen, that I try to hold onto it. I want to expand my ability to see the future as much as I can. I know; I complain about not having peace in my life, as I continuously try to expand my ability to connect to the energy that lives outside the physical.

I can't explain why I say this, but the truth is I feel obligated to stay connected. I feel there is some unknown reason for this ability that continues to grow along with me. I know there will come a day when I will understand why this energy is here.

Until that day comes, I will continue to learn and trust all that comes to me. It fascinates me. I trust its origin and the ability it offers me to know how both worlds can interact at any given moment.

If you can know the future once you can know it again. If I can develop my mind in the same way I can develop my body, I will have the ultimate machine of knowing and doing.

You can't learn what is offered to me from school, sports or anywhere other than in the present. To stay aware of the energy that coexists in the world we live in takes concentration.

I know the future starts in the present. The collective effect of all that is done now creates the conditions for the next right now.

Knowing this is why I can't just spin my wheels hoping someone else will get things done for me. Why a continued losing streak is unacceptable to me.

I make adjustments in my life to ensure I am connected to all avenues of learning, it's that important to me.

My instincts frequently guide me. I can't break away from them, when I try to, they only get stronger. If I doubt them, they prove me wrong. If I try to run from my guidance, it is right there at the end of my run.

I know it is odd to have such an unconventional way of living at this point in my life, but again all I can tell you is, I trust the energy that I have been given.

I feel it is there for a reason and I know if I were to lose it, I would be losing a large part of me.

Letting the force take me

Chapter 7

L ike I said to you in the previous chapter, the energy or force within my body pushes me. I find it to be so strong at times it over rules all that is going on around me.

I've decided to turn this trusted energy loose on my entire life. When I operate at my highest energy level it makes me feel ALIVE!!! The speed of information I receive and my being able to move physically at that speed, is freedom to me. When I stay aware of the present and allow it to guide my every moment my life is full..... So buckle up here it comes!!!

I return to my gym. I study and train and find my body expanding at warp speed. I search and find a weight lifters' doctor. He changes my diet and gives me a supplement to enhance my natural ability.

I meet with him in October weighing about 170lbs., In May I'm now 215lbs. I have been working out in my basement and have no real coach other than what I see, read and of course hear from within.

I've decided to enter the men's state bodybuilding contest. I take third place in the men's tall class, at seventeen years old.

The next week, I win the Teen Mr. East Coast. Not a bad eight days. Nice to win the second contest that I enter.

Nineteen months after walking off the football field, I am now the winner of all the East Coast. I have to keep what it is I'm doing kind of quiet because, well I'm still in high school and people think it's odd, including my father.

Do to the win; I am contacted by people in the sport. One of whom is a photographer I met when I won. He helps me gain more information and contacts. I go to meet with trainers in New York who have worked with many of the pros. They tell me to continue whatever it is I've been doing.

Fast forward one year, my basement gym is bursting out of the house and I am the youngest person ever to win, the AAU Mr. Massachusetts title. Onto the Teenage Mr. America, 2nd place, oh well. Politics!

I need a job! I receive a lot of attention because of the state title win. I get a certificate of achievement from the Governor of the state and a lot of press. Hmm, what to do?

I have been keeping an eye on an old sporting goods store across from City Hall for about two years now. When I walk by I instinctively peer into the windows. I went in the store a few times before it went out of business and always felt a strange connection to it.

I take the number of the landlord and call him to ask what the rental price is. He doesn't seem too crazy about talking business with an unemployed eighteen year old, but he tells me the rental price. I asked if I could see the place and we agree to meet this coming Saturday.

I tell my father what I'm up to and he's willing to go with me. Oh, by the way, I want to open a commercial gym on Main St. across from City Hall. No big deal right. I don't think so.

Saturday at 10:00 am my father and I meet the land lord at the empty building. They talk, and I ask questions. The land lord keeps talking to my father as though I'm not even there. I use this time to look around. Not bad, I can use the back of the store for a locker room and office.

The basement has plenty of room for storage and the structure of the main floor can hold all the weights without a problem. The sewer line is in the front of the building, so that's going to cost me a few extra bucks to tie into. All in all, I know I can make this work. I walk back over to the two of them, give my father a, I have made a decision nod, and I say to the land lord, "I'll take it."

The land lord looks, again, at my father and says, "Well you know I spoke to the owner in Boston and he told me he now wants an additional fifty dollars more per month."

I watch as my father looks down and I can tell he is thinking, well its people from Boston there's nothing I can do.

That's it, now I'm pissed and in a split second I think, look Mr. Land lord don't talk to him talk to me. Don't try to intimidate my father try intimidating me.

I take a breath and say, "Listen, this is my deal not his, you told me fifty dollars a month less on the phone. You tell Boston, I know this place has been empty for over two years. You tell Boston, I will be installing a completely upgraded plumbing system in this building at my cost."

I pull out the check that I have already written for the first month's rent and say to the land lord. "You take this check for the amount you originally told me, or tell, Boston the building is still empty".

He turns and faces me, looks back at my father, smiles and shrugs. My father is looking at him as if to say, oh I know, I live with him. I'm still fuming at the fact that he would not talk to me and that he tried to intimidate my father.

He takes the check, hands me the keys then says to me, "You'll need a plumbing permit for the work." My father stands up and says to him, "Don't worry, my father is the plumbing inspector." Good for you dad, take a swing at this guy.

Thirty days of nonstop work later, I open for business. I have the biggest, cleanest and most modern gym this city has ever seen and it's right on Main St., across from City Hall.

A few months later I get a call asking me to compete in a national qualifying contest; it's scheduled for April, in Florida.

The world wind of change that has been my last two years, coupled with the blizzard of 78, make it easy for me to say yes. I want to go to a warmer climate and take a break.

I ratchet up my training in preparation for April and as I do my business grows, but it is long hours. It seems all I do, is spend time at this gym and that's not me. So, I make about three phone calls and I have someone interested in buying my gym.

I'm having breakfast with my father when the phone rings and it's the buyer. My father hands me the phone with a strange look on his face.

I try to walk away to talk but the phone cord is not cooperating. I make the conversation as brief as possible and as I hang up, he is standing there stunned. He says, "You sold the gym?" I say, "Not yet."

April, I've arrive in Florida two weeks prior to the competition, all expenses paid. The gym is behind me. I am staying at the promoter's house with another bodybuilder who is here from Michigan. He is getting ready for the Mr. Universe contest. I'm here on a paid vacation. He goes to the gym and eats lettuce and chicken. I go to the gym and then sometimes, I go to Burger King. I keep feeling I'm in the wrong place. I just got to get out of here!

I'm offered a job and a place to live in Florida, but it's too hot for me here. I return to Mass. after the contest, repack my bags and move to Hollywood, Ca.

I have a job and the best of the best information right at my finger tips. My job is to build a gym with a man who is a friend of the photographers. No brainer for me.

I am slated to compete in the Teenage Mr. America in the summer. While I'm at the gym, Lou Ferrigno tells me to go apply for a job at Universal Studio, so I do. I get the job on the studio tour as the Incredible Hulk.

I have an agent come up to me and tell me he can get me work also. Next I find myself on the set of Welcome Back Kotter! John Travolta is walking down the hall towards me as I walk in.

The gym is now finished, but my boss is not happy with the outside success I've stumbled upon and oh yeah what was it I was doing? I remember, representing his gym in the Teenage Mr. America in Los Angeles.

The collective affect of all these avenues and what they bring with them, good and bad are taking a toll on me. I always felt I would be on TV and doing well, my grandfather had been telling me I would be on TV since I was about six years old. But the energy that is coming at me at this moment is way too much!

I hear that familiar voice warning me of going to deep into the Hollywood life style. I can feel I am right at the edge and if I jump, I will interfere with all that is meant to be.

So I stop, to protect an unknown future. A future that I know deep down inside is far more important than being a Hollywood actor. So for now it's back to Massachusetts to recharge, regroup and digest these last months of my life. The world got awfully big and it has been so mind blowing. I almost lost me.

I'm now running a construction crew and building a gym in the garage at my parent's house. My training partner and I have done a good job making this gym happen.

I find out that the Mr. USA competition is in NYC this year. I am presently Mr. New England which I won just a couple of months ago. So I think what the heck why not. I find out it is only eight weeks away, wow not much time. I enter and place 5th. Not bad, see a lot of people from Ca. who say come back out!

I think about it as winter nears. Again I feel the push, the knowing it's time to go.

Two weeks after I land in Ca. I get a part in Star Trek II the Wrath of Khan. Meant to be, what do you think?

This is how it goes at times, real smooth, and other times real rough. No other acting jobs come. I keep doing painting jobs and small home repair jobs.

I've decided to compete in the Mr. America that is up coming. I train for a few months and while doing so I suffer a nasty elbow injury that nearly ends my ability to weight lift. I am forced to stop. I ruptured the tendon in my right elbow.

I happen to meet a girl at the gym, who is a friend of a friend. We date and one day as I stand beside her I'm told, by that voice in my head, "She will give you the son you want."

Los Angeles is not where I want to raise my son. I became a Los Angeles County Sheriff before he was born and this environment is not where I want him to be. We decide to move back to the east coast.

Six years later, I am a Connecticut State Trooper; I have a five year old son and a divorce. I'm a single parent, and the courts pretty much cleaned me out, I am eventually forced into bankruptcy.

I continue acting and modeling out of NYC. The better I do in New York the more heat I catch at work. By 1990 I have won the Mr. Northeastern USA, heavy weight class. I have a manager out of NYC who wants me to drop fifty pounds and stop competing. What!?

New Years Eve 1990, while preparing to ring in the New Year, I get a call to return to Massachusetts because my mother is gravely ill. I drive from Conn. to Mass. and help my father and sister bring my mother immediately to the hospital.

I spend the next four days in the hospital waiting for the inevitable. As I sit beside my mother's death bed in her last hours of life, I hear her voice in my head, "Please stop competing and using steroids they are no good for you." I touch her hand and promise her I'll stop and I tell her it's time to let go of this life and not to fear the next.

My mother died tonight. I drive to my parent's house to get something from the house, what I don't know.

My sister is in the car with me, why, I don't know.

I normally don't carry a gun, but for some unknown reason when I looked up those steps at the door, I reached for my gun. I put the gun in the small of my back and watched the door as I approached. I've been on hot calls as a cop and this feels like a hot call to me.

I open the screen door and put my key in the lock and instinctively pull my gun out. The front door opens and there they are. Everywhere I look, there has to be at least a hundred people in the house waiting to know what is going on. They are up stairs looking down on me, to my right in the living room moving toward me, down the hall, in to the dining room, closing in on me. I point my gun at them all and say, "She's dead, now get the #@%# out of this house and leave us alone."

I stand in the entrance way and watch as these spirits move through walls, doors, windows, however it seems right for them. I just keep pushing them out with my energy until the last one is gone.

I feel it is so intrusive for these people to be in the house now. They are well dressed in clothes from the turn of the century and acting as if they were at a funeral with their somber looking faces as they leave the house.

I completely forget my sister is behind me. She doesn't say too much to me about it.

I told you this is a crazy house. Tonight it out did itself!

Less than two years later, I have a couple of movie parts behind me and a few national modeling jobs.

Today, I'm back in Massachusetts, this time I'm here to bury my father. He fought a heroic fight against cancer for years. He always did his best to make our family comfortable. He will be sadly missed.

After the funeral we all head back to my parent's house, well now it's our house, the four of us. We are the older generation, just like that.

When my sisters and I are all back in the house it's strange, the energy in the house is obviously final. My mother was 56 when she died, now my father at 60, way too young, way too young.

It is with a heavy heart that I think of my life at this moment. So much loss, so much pain and now I no longer have parents.

Allowing the energy in my life to guide me has given me experiences that I otherwise would not have had. The lessons I've learned and the education I have gained do to this force within me are priceless.

I am thirty four years old now. I will not turn my back on my guidance just because it has been rough at times. I still trust the peaceful sound that I hear coming from within.

My parents left this earth at a young age. Everyone's life has an expiration date, knowing this actually reinforces my resolve to continue living in both worlds the way that I do.

People tell me I have a gift, all I can say is, I hope so.

A Gift?

Chapter 8

I certainly don't remember asking for this gift! Would you call the things that I experience a gift?

Whose idea was it to give this to me anyway? Maybe it was the same person who put the St. Jude picture in my room.....

Ok I get it, not everyone can see the things I do, but I suspect there is a reason for this ability, is there not? Maybe not but, I feel there is a responsibility on my part to use this for the good.

What is odd though is there are times when this gift scares people; it can cause isolation, and it can create questions about the origin of the information.

I often have people say they would love to be able to do what I do. To do what I do starts with being given the ability in the first place. The next hurdle is, trying to understand what is going on; not an easy thing to wrap the mind around. Think about it, there are instruction booklets given to us when we buy a toaster. No instruction booklet comes with this.

I have developed my ability over the many years by learning how to recognize when information comes to me. I've learned to listen to my guidance above my own thoughts. You know what I mean? For example if I'm at the store and think: let me get a loaf of bread, I might hear: you don't need it, and every time I go ahead and buy the loaf of bread anyway, I end up throwing it out.

It takes discipline to adhere to the guidance that comes to me. This guidance is the constant stream of energy that flows through my head. I don't think many people would want the constant buzzing in their head twenty four hours a day seven days a week or the energy drain that it causes. These are part of the costs of having this ability.

Over the years I've also developed an ability to do readings for people. Some call them psychic readings or clairvoyant readings. I feel it is just another form of the ability, or gift.

Like anything else there can be good and bad associated with predicting the future. I have heard people say it is wrong to do such a thing. I have had people ask me if I am demonic. Honestly, I laugh every time and immediately tell them, "No I'm a good guy."

While doing my research for this book, I came across a very well known book that supports my belief. I believe that my ability or gift is in no way wrong or rooted in evil. I found out that one of the most popular religious figures of the past two thousand plus years was able to predict the future. His name was Jesus Christ.

Yes, that's what I just said, Jesus was psychic....

The book that I learned this from is called the Holy Bible. If you don't believe me then go to the book of Mathew 24-26.This book is where you find that Jesus told his apostles, he will be crucified in fulfillment of the scriptures!

He told Judas at the last supper that he would betray him and after betraying him he would regret it. Well Judas did turn Jesus over to the Romans and shortly after he hanged himself out of despair.

Jesus went on to tell Peter, before the cock crows he would deny Jesus three times, which Peter did. Jesus told his apostles there would be wars over his preaching. There have not only been the Holy Wars he was referring to but, religious wars are still going on as of today.

Obviously Jesus did much more than predict the future he was able to heal people also. He made the blind man see and the crippled man walk, to name a few. His ability came from God. Jesus was psychic, he was a healer and he was a Prophet.

The source of communication that someone like Jesus used still remains today. Meaning the source that Jesus used to perform such actions did not leave the universe because he did. It was here before him and after him.

I understand clearly I am not Jesus and the ability to heal people that I have experienced doesn't equate in any way to him. The point I am trying to make is healing, predicting and other spiritual abilities are gifts given to some. What someone does with this type of gift is up to the individual.

I chose to develop my gifts and they have improved greatly over time. I can honestly say I have healed people both physically and emotionally.

Clairvoyance is described as having the ability to receive information from the divine. That might sound a little pompous but the truth is it has to come from somewhere.

Remember Jesus and people before him had the ability to be Prophets so it's been around since the beginning of man. I realize the ability to see, hear or be guided instantly is truly a gift. The ability to heal is an incredible gift. I can use the energy in my hands to help heal certain people. The more I practice this, the better I become at it.

I'm aware of the need to share what it is I know at times for the benefit of others. I've been doing readings for over twenty years. Whenever I do a reading for someone I pray or meditate for a period before I start. I ask for protection and truth to be present. I don't do readings for too many people because they are very personal to the person being read and it never really became a large part of my life. I get a lot of joy from helping people get back on track.

Most of the readings that I have done are more of a self help or guidance style of reading. I have done many readings when relatives or friends who have passed on come through.

I try to help people on both sides come to peace with their loss. I don't do the, where did Uncle Frank hide the jewelry kind of thing. I don't want to cheapen the ability I've been given.

I know that when I crawl into someone's life and help them, than yes it is a gift. I want the gift to be only used for positive change. I always want to help people find their peace. Often times it is a painful process for them.

Change can be painful. I find one of the ways people hold on to lost loved ones is guilt. Often time's guilt is the way we keep the memory alive. That's not healthy. Guilt is not a healthy way to hold on to anyone.

I have felt what people who have passed on feel during these readings and quite frankly it is almost always love and forgiveness. Whether they are giving it or wanting it, it seems those are the bulk of the feelings present.

The thing I try to get people to understand is that the person who has left you is still that person. So if you're loved one acted a certain way while on the earth this is still who they are after passing.

I'm also asked if it scares me to see or communicate with the other world. I'm not afraid because I know they are just people. Strangers don't scare me, dead or alive. Like the many people who were in my parents' home the night my mother died. For all I know those people could have all been my relatives who came to comfort me. I didn't feel like making introductions at the time.

If you think it may be a surprising event for me to have contact with the other side then go back and reread chapter 2.

When I do a reading I am able to spend some time with the participants on both sides of the universe. So I am able to get a truer feel for what is being said. Remember it really is a matter of being able to connect to existing energy.

The other side of the coin is I can't just continuously tell the future because I'll have no present.

When I'm out in public there are times when I hear things about strangers who are near me. For example if I'm in a store I may hear one word of information that pertains to the person walking past me. I often times hear things about an individual's health, like cancer, or heart attack. I'll sometimes hear of emotional issues people are having too such as suicidal or feelings of being unloved.

I can't tell everyone one what I hear. I would be locked up as a crazy man if I stood there letting it all out. Could you imagine the interference this would cause in people's lives?

The simple explanation of these events is the information never stops!!!

I need to be away from crowds because of this occurrence. It is not as overwhelming as say that first day of school, but it is there. The gift that people so badly want to have comes with unrelenting conditions.

I do apply my gift to my own life as you know. Often times without knowing just how it will turn out. The force I spoke about that pushes me, is part of the gift.

The protection I have been given at times, when honestly, I could have been badly injured or killed is of great importance to me also. Yeah, the benefit of instant information has undoubtedly saved my life more than once.

A gift? I would have to say, yes.

Looking through my eyes

Chapter 9

B y now you must have a good understanding of how my life is.

In this chapter I want to share with you just a few of the many experiences that I have had over these years. I call it looking through my eyes because I want you to see it as I did!

I have worked as a commercial print model since the seventies. Today, I'm working for Talk magazine in New York City. It's an early September day. I'm at a roof top studio on the west side, right off the West Side Highway. It is down near Eighteenth Ave. right on the Hudson River.

The shoot starts at about nine in the morning, and it is scheduled to go for God knows how long. It shouldn't be that long, besides we have access to a roof top restaurant and outside bar, how bad can it be?

I feel a need to go out onto the roof and look out over the water, or south towards the lower part of Manhattan as often as time allows.

Initially, I find it to be quiet refreshing to go out and watch the boats on the Hudson River during the short breaks. As the morning lingers on the weather outside starts to get cloudy, but I don't mind, I continue to go out onto the roof. I notice as the afternoon approaches I am having intermittent feelings of sadness when I look south towards the financial center, odd.

We break for lunch around two o'clock, and I can't help but notice the feeling of sadness I have when looking south. It is now a constant and it is getting stronger.

I think, maybe I'm feeling sad because I'm stuck on this job for way too long and for very little money. No, that's not it; this is way too deep of a feeling to just be about the crappy pay.

It starts to rain by mid afternoon. I find myself slipping deeper and deeper into a state of sadness as I look out the windows. I no longer want to look out over the water. I am drawn to the southern side of the building, and my gaze is narrowing on to the World Trade Center.

Back inside I go for yet another round of pictures. The pictures are a group shot of military guys all huddled around this tall brunette model with crazy hair, it's an editorial shot.

We all talk with each other in between set ups. I meet a guy who is upset because he has to pick up his daughter after school and it is now way past that time. He made arrangements for her to go to his mother's house, so she is ok, but he now is worried about getting a cab and all this other stuff. I tell him I would be happy to give him a ride at the end of the day.

We shoot another round of pictures and are given another break. By now it's raining so hard I can't see too far south, but the sadness is even stronger. I stand here looking out the window trying to understand why I feel this way. Is it the rain? I find my eyes again fixating on the World Trade Center. I feel such sadness looking at the Twin Towers.

By seven pm we are all done shooting. Thank God, what a long day! I find my friend who needs a ride, and we head down to the parking garage inside the building. I give the attendant my ticket and they charge me a third of my pay for the day to park!! Aghhhhh, what a day!

I'm sad looking out the window, I just got ripped off by the parking company and now it's raining so hard that traffic is at a standstill. It takes me twenty minutes just to go three blocks.

My friend is obviously concerned about his daughter so I try to keep my frustration to myself.

I keep thinking about the sadness I felt when I looked at the World Trade Center. I can feel the stress of people trying to get through the heavy traffic on their way home. I am getting images of people trying to flee the city. I turn to my friend and say, "Could you imagine what would happen if this city were ever in need of evacuation?" He says "Oh, I know it would be really difficult to get everyone out all at once."

I drop him off at the address he needed and decided to take Riverside Drive north, finally heading home. I can't wait to get out of here. I feel a sense of urgency to get as far away from this place as possible.

I happened to check the clock on the dash board of my car and it was about eight pm. September 10th 2001.

Within fourteen hours the World Trade Center would be under attack, three thousand people would be dead and people would be running from the city……

Sadness was all around me before it even happened. The mad dash to get out of the city was flashing in my mind.

I was taking down a small addition on a house I once lived in. I was at the point where the frame for the roof was ready to be taken down. Being handy and cheap, I was doing the bulk of the demolition myself.

I realized I could reach the roof rafters by standing inside the room I was taking down. I started up my chain saw and was preparing to cut the first rafter from the wall when I felt a need to stop. I waited for a second and then lifted my saw up over my head to make the first cut. As I lifted the saw I heard a calm male voice, I think was my father, say, "Step back one bay." I stepped back one bay and began cutting the original beam I intended to cut just a moment ago. As the saw cut threw, the triangular beam fell right in front of my face and slammed onto the ground. It missed my face by inches, had I been standing in the place I was originally, it would have come down and crushed the side of my head. I'm sure it would have killed me...

Thanks dad! By the way he was not alive at this time.

I was working the evening shift as a State Trooper one Sunday when four of us decided to meet up for dinner. The traffic on Sundays is usually light and this day was no different.

The weather was clear and it was a warm early summer day. Being on the road for hours and not having a bathroom available we all head to the men's room to freshen up. I was standing in front of the urinal when I had a strong feeling of energy come over me. I finished, stepped back and as I did I realized there was going to be a fatal accident.

I looked around the room at each Trooper hearing "Nope, not him." until the energy settled on one of them. I stopped at the guy who was my wing man. I said, "Hey there is going to be a fatal accident soon and it is going to be yours." He just looked at me like I was nuts.

We all went back to the table and I told the waitress to hurry up because we had to go. When the food came out I could feel the energy climb. I told them they better eat quickly because we didn't have much time. The three of them just shrugged me off. I know how long it takes to process a fatal accident, so I put the last bite of food in my mouth as the radio called out my wing mans call numbers. He was told there was a possible fatal accident at such and such a location. Off we went....

It was a fatal accident, one car, one man, on a perfectly clear day. Cops don't get me.

My son had to have a dog!!! He had to have a Boxer! So guess what, life brought him a boxer. Good for him, he's a good kid a great student, a polite child and his parents are divorced. Max is the dogs name and he is the nicest dog you'll ever find.

The only problem is as he gets older he just takes off. It seemed almost only on Sundays. We sometimes spend hours if not the whole day looking for that dog.

Those of you who have dogs know you worry that they might not return. You worry they might get hit by a car and you feel bad that your child will have to suffer a loss. So what do you do? You drive around looking for the animal, blindly.

This activity went on for YEARS! We moved and it seemed to stop, only briefly. One Sunday I realized he was gone, again. We get into the truck and as I back out I hear, "North West."

The truck has a compass on the rear view mirror and as I backed out it read east. I pulled out onto the road and it read north. I knew west was to my left so I went left. Now the compass read west. I got to an intersection and heard, "Left." I turned left and the compass read south. I went about a half a mile and heard, "Right." I took a right and the compass read west. AHHH!! Still no Max! What am I doing? I continue about half a block and I hear, "Take a right and go straight."

Ok, now I think I'm losing my mind! Just as I take the right and go about one hundred yards, I check the compass and it flips to northwest, I look away from the compass, just having watched it turn from west to northwest and here comes Max. He ran right out in front of the truck.

Trusting the incoming information can be difficult!!

About a year or so after my mother died, I was still torn with the idea of continuing with bodybuilding or not. I was torn between acting or not. I was unsure about continuing to be a police officer or not.

I was on patrol near my apartment towards the end of an evening shift one night. I decided to make a quick stop and check my answering machine and most likely grab a bite to eat. There were no messages, so I went back on the road. My son had left some school supplies at a friend's house who watched him for me this day. I called and later stopped by after my shift was over to grab the things he left behind.

The woman and I both worked in the same building and our sons were about the same age so we were aware of each other's day to day.

I was talking with her about the multiple cross roads I felt I was at. I was saying how I'm in need of guidance through this time. As I was getting ready to leave I said, "It would be nice if I could play the game you're hot, you're cold." We laughed and I left. On my way back home I was thinking about that game and how it would really be helpful if there was someone there to tell me at every step you're hot or cold.

I arrived home within minutes after having that conversation. I checked my answering machine and noticed it was flashing "1". I remember thinking; it's late who could have called? I pushed the play button and started to take my uniform off. The tape rewound and then the most eerie, never heard before sound came out of the speakers. It started with a whooshing / electrical / out of space sound, as the sound go louder or closer, I heard a voice.

This voice was VERY familiar! The message was: Hh.. Hhou... Hot! (Click) silence. It took the caller three tries to get out the word, HOT. I immediately fell to my knees and felt as though I was exposed to the entire universe, as if there was no place to hide! I can't explain it better than being completely exposed! The voice on the answering machine was my MOTHER!!!

My mother left me a message from beyond this world...

I've mentioned that I have information or premonitions come to me at times through dreams. One morning just before I woke up I had a dream of a building that is under construction. In my dream, I was looking at the roof of a commercial building that was newly framed out. In the dream as I was standing there looking at the structure of the roof it collapsed.

It was like a domino effect, the roof rafters suddenly fell from right to the left. The peak fell to the left then one after another until the entire roof was gone. It took about fifteen seconds. I could hear it in my dream. I could smell the freshly cut wood.

When I woke up, I went about my usual routine then left for work. I always stop at the same store for coffee and the paper on the way in to work. Today is no different. I paid for my things and as I turned to exit, I realized there was a building under construction right across the street.

The roof had been framed, it seemed over night! It stopped me dead in my tracks to look at that building. As I stood there looking at the roof, it happened.

The wind blew and the roof collapsed from right to left one section at a time until it was completely gone. I could hear each section smack the next. When I stepped outside to get in my car the air was filled with the smell of freshly cut wood. In this case it was freshly splintered wood.

From dream to reality.

I signed on one morning when I was a police officer and was immediately ordered to go to a missing person, scene. I acknowledged the call and asked for details. I thought maybe I would see the person on the way to it. I was told to go to the house and report to the supervisor at the scene for details.

Ok, when I turned on to the street there were cops all over the place. There must have been ten police vehicles at the house. I saw blood hounds and German shepherds and about ten cops. I remember thinking, wow who are we looking for the president?

I walked into the house and reported to the officer in charge. He pretty much said get out of our way. He said, "We have been here all night; we have a room covered in blood and a missing man, we are not sure if this is a crime scene or not".

I told him I was there to assist in any way I could and to let me know if they needed help. He went back to the men he was working with and left me standing there.

The house was pumped up with energy from all these cops and frantic family members. It just didn't match up to the feeling of calm that I was feeling. I placed my hands in my pockets, cop thing, no prints, and decided to take a look around for myself.

I went to the room covered in blood first. I thought I would learn something from the blood pattern or pooling or whatever. Yeah there was blood there, but it didn't have the look of a struggle. I didn't feel a crime had taken place. I was actually feeling weak as if I was dizzy from the loss of blood.

I was then drawn to the bathroom, more blood and again I have a feeling of weakness.

I went to the living room and everything I was feeling left me. I decided to go to the kitchen to see what I would feel there.

The kitchen felt the same as the living room, nothing urgent. As I walked away from the kitchen I heard a voice say, "Doctor."

When I heard that I was guided to the phone on the wall in the hallway. I looked at this old green wall phone and right on top of the phone, I found a piece of paper with big numbers on it. It's a phone number, so I picked up the phone and dialed the number.

The phone rang about three times before being answered. I hear a woman answer the phone and say, "St. Mary's Hospital", I said, "Hi can you tell me if, (our guy) has recently been admitted to your hospital? I was transferred to patient information and repeated my question. The person on the other end of the phone said, "Yes, he came in during the night."

I thanked them for the information and hung up. I looked around through the many cops and dogs buzzing around and saw the supervisor who had just moments ago told me they had it all under control.

I calmly worked my way over to him and quietly said, "I found him." He turned and looked at me as if to say who are you again? I said it again, "I found him, and he is at St. Mary's hospital where he has been all night." As he called out to all his men to stop the search, I got in my car and drove off. They were there for hours; I was there about fifteen minutes....

It's nice to have help!

I have a friend who owns his own business. He is in the construction field and therefore his work is very labor intensive. He has a large family who depend on him to survive. He is also active in martial arts. One evening during his workout he heard a loud pop come from his knee.

He was in enough pain to seek medical attention. He was sent to an orthopedic surgeon for further examination. The orthopedic doctor told him he needed to have surgery immediately to repair the injury.

During the operation he somehow contacted an infection in the knee. He ended up back in the hospital sick and in a lot of pain.

After a few weeks I heard he was home so, I decided to stop by and see him. When I got there he and his wife were in the kitchen and they were visibly upset. He had just returned from the surgeon's office where he had his last visit. I was surprised to see he was still on crutches.

I asked how things were going and they were both near tears as they told me the doctor said he would never walk without crutches again. I looked at him and that force in me just made me say, "What, he's an idiot I don't believe that."

They both looked at me like I was not listening. They said it again, "the doctor told me I would never walk again." I said, "He's wrong I don't believe that."

I just couldn't accept that this information was correct. I felt it to the depths of my soul. I asked him if he would allow me to check his leg out. He stood there on his crutches while I basically tried to straighten his leg. While I was doing this a few of his children came into the kitchen. I was able to get his leg to straighten out and as I did I took his crutches away. He stood there for a moment and I told him to walk to me, which he did.

I looked around the room and his family members all started crying because he was able to walk again. I went on working on him for a few more weeks. I would mostly bury my thumbs into the congested tissue while forcing energy into the leg. He now has about 98% of his ability back in that leg.

Healing hands or thick head?

I had a woman ask me if I would do a reading for her. I agreed to do it for her and made arraignments for her to meet with me at my work. There is a back room with a table and chairs so it is easy for me to do it there.

She is coming in at four in the afternoon. From where I sit at work I can see down the hall to the back room and see the chairs back there.

At around 3:00 pm I noticed the spirit of an elderly woman sitting in the back room waiting. After a little time passed she started saying the name, "Kitty" to me. Every time I looked down the hall, I would see her sitting there all dressed up in a skirt and blazer, purse resting on her lap. She would look right at me and without moving a muscle. I would hear her repeatedly say, "Kitty, Kitty." I had no idea what her being there was about, but I assumed she was there for the woman coming in at 4:00 pm. I have had people show up for readings in the past so I wasn't too surprised.

When four o'clock came Karen walked in. I walked with her to the back and had her sit at the table I had set up. As she sat down I watched the woman turn in her chair to face Karen.

I had Karen shuffle the cards and return them to me. I spread the cards out and before I began, I said, "I don't know what this means to you but there is a woman sitting behind you who has been here for about an hour. I described the woman to her and Karen seemed a little upset. I then said, "She keeps calling you Kitty."

When she heard me say that name she burst out crying!

I sat there with her and gave her some Kleenex. The woman stood up, moved closer and put her left hand on Karen's shoulder, the woman looked at me and said, "Tell her it's ok."

I never know what is going on between people at times like these so I try to slow the process down to find out. I told her the woman was touching her shoulder and saying it's ok.

That didn't seem much comfort so I just sat there and told her again the woman is with her. After about five minutes Karen was able to tell me the woman was her mother. Ah ha.

Karen then apologized for getting so upset. She explained that her mother had died while Karen was in a hospital out of state and confined to bed. She explained how it had bothered her all these years because she never got to say good bye. Her mother died and was buried while she was confined to a hospital bed out of state.

It was unimaginable to see how the spirit of this mother stayed with her daughter. Karen told me she knew as soon as I said, Kitty that it was her mother, because no one else ever called her that, only her mother.

They seemed to make peace, and I did the reading. The mother left as soon as her daughter was calm.

The closure that was given to these two women was amazing.

Throughout the years I have met with many types of people. I have had people come to me who are far more educated than I am, but they can't seem to put their life in order. What I am able to do is remove the chaos from their mind. I am able to show people how to get their mind at a place where it all makes sense again.

I had a man I worked with once who has a degree in law and another degree in finances. One of the most highly educated people I have ever worked with.

This particular man could not break from the constant confusion in his head. These thoughts were so fast and so random that he became trapped in his own head. His mind was a play ground for irrational thinking. He lived in a state of chaos. He couldn't put one clear thought next to another. His education seemed of no use to him, so why even try. It was shocking to me how such an educated man could become so paralyzed by his mind.

During our conversations I would see bits and pieces of his childhood. I would tell him what I was seeing and that one of his uncles was coming to me. I would tell him I could hear the uncle telling him, "One day the family business would all be yours."

We realized after a few meetings was he was still trying to please his family and not himself. He was trapped in all that was said to him as a boy. I told him his uncle wanted him to break free from his promises that he made as a child. He was able to recall the experiences I spoke to him about. He eventually made peace with his past promises and freed himself from the burden of living in the past.

The realization that he didn't have to continue the family business was the key that unlocked his imprisoned mind. With that he smiled and left. I heard from him about a year later. He called to thank me and to tell me he has a great job and bought a home of his own.

If it wasn't for his uncle coming through to say to him, "It's ok not to live by your childhood promises," he would never have let go of the guilt.

These are just a few of the ways I can use my abilities to help others.

The Present

Chapter 10

T he way I live has given me a unique way of dealing with the world around me. Knowing that information is available to me in the present is a tool I use often. I know we can all receive information in the present if we are able to calm the mind and not interfere with the process. This is obviously not an adjustment that can be made over night. It has to become part of your instincts.

I truly believe that everyone can enhance their life by listening to the guidance that is available to each of us. The amount of information will vary of course from person to person, based on ability and practice.

One of the difficulties is, knowing what is real and what wishful thinking is. You know, like when you have a thought and you kind of talk yourself into believing it's real, as opposed to knowing and feeling the truth of the thought. I always say you really don't know until you're on the other side of it. Meaning the information that comes to you may be less clear until it becomes a known. Repetition is the only way to recognize the subtlety between the two. This repetition can take years.

The constant day to day, of making a living and caring for our families consumes our time and our thoughts. Remember we all have the mental capacity to do many things at once. The science of the mind has estimated that we only use a small portion of our brain in our life time. So why not tap into the part of our mind that is the most useful.

Staying in the present and concentrating on listening while living is a tough change to make. Not everyone can stay in the present twenty four hours a day. I know how important it is and it is truly difficult for me at times.

The lesson I have learned is fight back to now at all costs because it is the best place to begin a correction. What I mean by this is right here right now, this moment.

Fears, anger, all the emotions that interrupt our present, push us off track. These emotions can drive us or they can also be misleading.

Often I explain it by using a long stick. You anchor one end of a stick in place. Then angle it one way or another. The opposite end of the stick moves greatly in comparison to the anchored end. A very minor adjustment at the present has a very dramatic out come in the future.

The toughest point in your life can be altered if you can stay now. It's like when you are injured, the immediate response of the body is to go into shock. Shock consolidates and prioritizes the needs of the body. The physical instincts of the body, in times of shock, are a protective state of being in the present. The body won't allow you to feel the intense pain because it's focused on healing. The awareness of the pain will interrupt this immediate response which is vital for the body to heal. The body instinctively knows what to do and we can't interrupt it.

Why not accept a similar condition to instinctively guide the brain. Stop trying to live tomorrow, when today is still here. Try not to stay in yesterday while missing today.

It is not easy to do. The past is real and it has affected us in many ways. The future doesn't exist yet, but we must prepare for it. What we do with this information is important; it will help or hinder our progress depending on our thinking.

We know what to do physically when there is a problem, fix it! If you're bleeding your focus is to stop the bleeding. We don't sit there saying wow look at all that blood loss...... because we will bleed to death. When the bleeding has stopped then it's time to rest and rebuild our blood supply.

The mind can be used in a similar way. Stop the bleeding, calm the mind. Listen to the thoughts that are present, and know they are there for a reason.

Where do you think your physical instincts come from anyway? They come from the mind, your mind. The mind that instinctively tells you to pull your hand away from a hot stove. We don't doubt the physical instincts because we trust them to help us.

Allow the mental instincts to do the same. What you need to do is to develop them much in the same way you learned how to trust the physical.

We have all said this, "I knew I shouldn't have done it, but I did it anyway." That's interfering with your mental instincts. This is the slight turn of the anchored stick that moves the far end a great distance.

Remember, information is energy. The human mind receives and transmits energy, so make good use of it.

As I mentioned it is not an easy process. The altering of one's thought process takes time and energy. The good thing is nobody has to know your altering your train of thoughts but you. It will only become apparent to others when you become a more peaceful more knowing person. The best part about it is it's free!

Be patient with this because it is not an immediate condition. It will take some energy to get there. It will take some time to get there, but in the end, it's yours to keep. No one can take it from you and it will only improve with time.

The brain is physical and part of our bodies. If your body is polluted or sick it won't function at its best. It's the same with the brain.

The physical condition of the body does dictate the speed and ability of the mind. The greater the speed of the brain is, the better the connection is. So make sure as you work your way towards learning how to better use your mind, you take into full account just how important your health is in the equation. Healthy body, healthy mind and with these two entities working at maximum capacity, watch out world here you come!

I don't want to go too far into this aspect of broadening the mind, but remember to protect yourself. Keep your thoughts positive so you will always be taping into a positive informational source. Start teaching that new section of your mind to only respond to the positive.

We all can achieve a more capable body and mind if we choose to. Diet and exercise are essential to the overall success of your transformation. So stay at it every day, step by step and watch as you become a more knowing, healthy person.

Both worlds, physical and spiritual can work together; they are here with you already. Why not take advantage of them?

Both Worlds

Chapter 11

"Both Worlds!"

They're **waiting** *for you!*

CPSIA information can be obtained at www.ICGtesting.com
Printed in the USA
LVOW07s1553201215

467301LV00003B/449/P